chris rea

piano/vocal/guitar tablature

Folio © 1994 International Music Publications Limited
Southend Road, Woodford Green, Essex IG8 8HN England
Music Transcribed by Barnes Music Engraving Ltd.,
East Sussex TN22 4HA
Photos by Stephen Sandon
Printed by Panda Press · Haverhill · Suffolk CB9 8PR

215-2-1123

espresso logic

chris rea

biography

1972	Aged 21 buys guitar.
1973	Signs first publishing deal. "To someone from an industrial northern town where recession is hitting hard and fast it seemed like a good deal! You live and learn."
1974-76	The dole. Plus "other" jobs. Local bands etc.
1977	1st album. "Hate it, hated doing it, I thought every-one worked like that, soon found out."
1978	Hit single Fool If You Think It's Over. Top 10 USA for five weeks. Grammy nomination for Best Newcomer.
1979	2nd album as contracted, "nothing to do with what I wanted to do. Knew then I wasn't ever going to be a rock star, but knew how much I loved music and writing".
1980	Tennis, highly acclaimed, self-produced using old band from home; sold zero.
1980	Manipulated into fourth album "me versus the star makers. They thought they'd won when the record was finished but they hadn't, the record flopped - no winners anywhere."
1981	Decides to give up on "the business" side. His wife convinces him to carry on but start again and move to London.
1982	Dave Pennyfeather finds a 'demo album' decides to give it a try in Ireland. Big hit in Ireland and Germany. Rea finds new management and "invents" a family business of "Hotel Rea" records and tours only.
1983	More fights with the business, this time over Bombollini on Wired To The Moon. An ethnic epic which had a six minute video script but "they" wanted 3 mins.
1984	Shamrock Diaries - suddenly championed by journalists and coupled with lots of gigs things get better for "Hotel Rea" although still many hundreds of thousands of pounds in debt. Rea (now a father) says he's getting happy.
1985-86	On The Beach. Now working with the famed Max Middleton (keyboards) and Martin Ditcham (drums/percussion). "Learnt a lot off Max (and still do)." Still plagued by the "normal rock way of doing things". "Cry, shout, laugh - move on."
Late '80s	Acclaimed Dancing With Strangers breaks new ground and although his succcss has been growing strongly in Europe since Watersign (1982), starts to become popular in the UK, to the effect of his contract being sold (unbeknownst to him) to Warner Brothers who release a "Best Of" which Rea re-records at his own expense with his regular musicians.

The Road To Hell
Autobiographical account of life on the gravy train. Struck a chord with every person in the world who had to leave what they loved in order to survive in the late eighties only to find out it wasn't the answer.

Auberge
Similar continued success. His own home-movie a big success.

God's Great Banana Skin
"The lack of comment (good or bad) about unique exploratory tracks such as 'Miles Was A Cigarette' and 'Nothing To Fear' was worrying to say the least." - CR

Espresso Logic
Less than a full year later!

"I'm ready to start a new album tomorrow." -CR

Very different from the last three albums. Rea seems to be starting to be himself without apologising.

In process:- 3 film scripts, 4 film scores, 2 book commissions and a piece of music that is so far already two and a half hours long and a duet with Elton John...watch this space...

"A complex symphony of contradictions," is a quote Rea strongly disagrees with: "Creating music and lyrics and not being a pop/rock star has NEVER been a contradiction," he says, "to say you must be both is a very narrow, unrealistic and lazy statement and in this day and age has surely become an out of date concept anyway."

Rea has suffered more than most for being his own man saying that it has always been frustrating and perplexing to have to work in the constraints and bureaucracy of the 'rock business' which he compares humorously to "a bunch of cardinals in Rome, making rules for the sake of their own being."

Critics and record producers have struggled for over ten years now to stick him in a category of some kind, only to be once again perplexed at his next release. Rea is constantly looking out to sea and shows no signs of having any inclination whatsoever of looking back to shore.

His new album, "Espresso Logic", gives verification of this, opening with an Irish Italian melody that runs into a piece written for the Uillean pipes (played by Davy Spillane), finishing up somewhere between Brazil and Italy, using "real" musicians (almost unique in this day and age). He takes "themes of the modern struggle" and turns them into rhythm, melody and lyrics.

There is no parody or pastiche of rock/pop images here. "Some critics and producers have always wrongfully mistaken melody for 'softness'; something they will be challenged with on judgement day!" And to confound all and sundry yet again, he ends the album with a live club song which finishes up as a poem set against the sound of the sea. Definitely different.

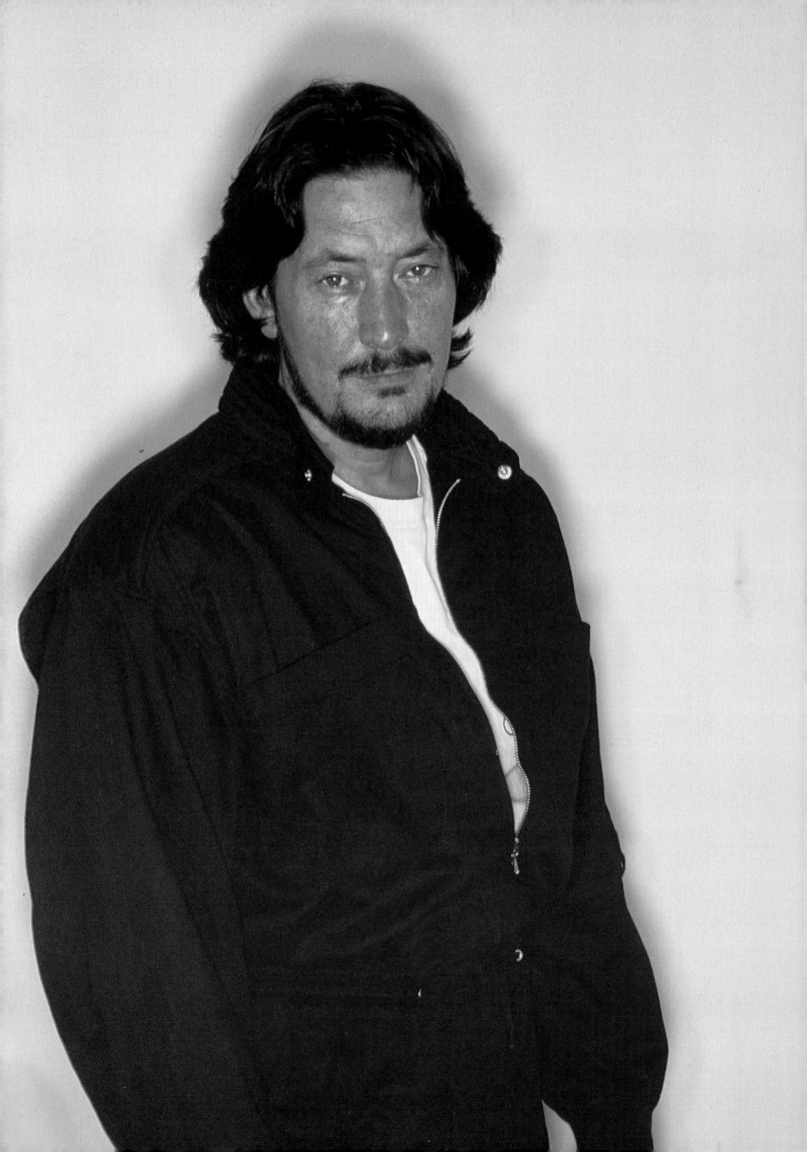

Notation and Tablature Explained

Diese Erklärungen erscheinen am Ende des Buches in deutsch.

Vous trouverez la traduction française de ces instructions à la fin du livre.

Open C chord

Scale of E major

High E (1st) string
B (2nd) string
G (3rd) string
D (4th) string
A (5th) string
Low E (6th) string

Bent Notes:

The note fretted is always shown first. Variations in pitch achieved by string bending are enclosed within this symbol ⌐ ¬ . If you aren't sure how far to bend the string, playing the notes indicated without bending gives a guide to the pitches to aim for. The following examples cover the most common string bending techniques:

Example 1:
Play the D, bend up one tone (two half-steps) to E.

Example 4:
Pre-bend: fret the D, bend up one tone to E, then pick.

Example 2:
Play the D, bend up one tone to E then release bend to sound D. Only the first note is picked.

Example 5:
Play the A and D together, then bend the B-string up one tone to sound B.

Example 3:
Fast bend: Play the D, then bend up one tone to E as quickly as possible.

Example 6:
Play the D and F♯ together, then bend the G-string up one tone to E, and the B-string up ½ tone to G.

Additional guitaristic techniques have been notated as follows:

Mutes
a) Right hand mute:
Mute strings by resting the right hand on the strings just above the bridge.
b) Left hand mute:
Damp the strings by releasing left hand pressure just after the notes sound.
c) Unpitched mute:
Damp the strings with the left hand to produce a percussive sound.

Hammer on and Pull off:
Play first note, sound next note by 'hammering on', the next by 'pulling off'. Only the first note is picked.

Tremolo Bar:
Alter pitch using tremolo bar. Where possible, the pitch to aim for is shown.
a) Play the G; use the bar to drop the pitch to E.
b) Play the open G; use the bar to 'divebomb', i.e. drop the pitch as far as possible.

Glissando:
a) Play first note, sound next note by sliding up string. Only the first note is picked.
b) As above, but pick second note.

Slide Guitar:
a) Play using slide.
b) Play without slide.

Vibrato:
Apply vibrato, by 'shaking' note or with tremolo bar. As vibrato is so much a matter of personal taste and technique, it is indicated only where essential.

Pinch Harmonics:
Fret the note as usual, but 'pinch' or 'squeeze' the string with the picking hand to produce a harmonic overtone. Small notes show the resultant pitch.

Quarter-tones:
A downwards arrow means the written pitch is lowered by a quarter-tone; an upwards arrow raises the written pitch by a quarter-tone.

Special Tunings:
Non-standard tunings are shown as 'tuning boxes'. Each box represents one guitar string, the leftmost box corresponding to the lowest pitched string. The symbol '•' in a box means the pitch of the corresponding string is not altered. A note within a box means the string must be re-tuned as stated. For tablature readers, numbers appear in the boxes. The numbers represent the number of half-steps the string must be tuned up or down. The tablature relates to an instrument tuned as stated.

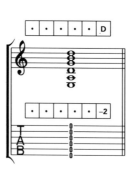

Tune the top E (1st) string down two semitones (two half-steps) to D. See 'Espresso Love.'

espresso logic

if you don't listen what the people say
the people gonna have to take their own way
you got to give the people what they need
and only then will they begin to see

there's a world that we don't know
there's a world we never see
espresso

i don't need this trouble
i don't need the grief
i don't need to feel this pressure down on me
everyday there's something we don't really need
stop think
walk away and let it be
stop think
walk away and let it be

espresso logic

Words & Music by
Chris Rea

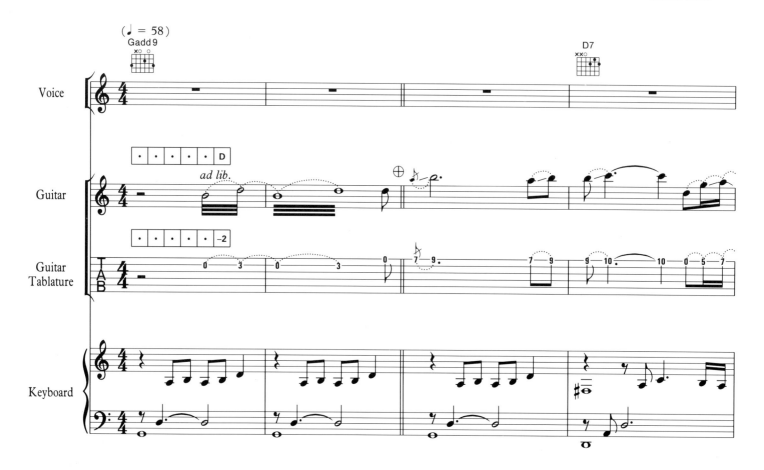

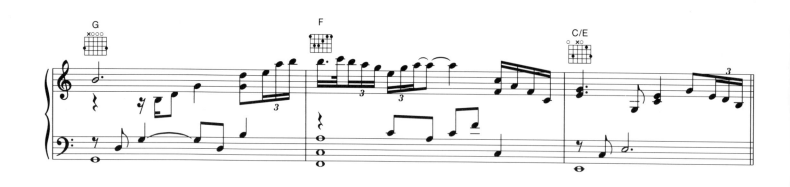

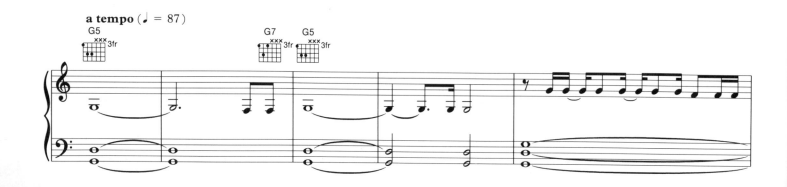

you don't lis - ten what the peo - ple say,___ the peo - ple gon - na have to take their own

walk a-way and let it be,__ stop, think, walk a-way and let it be.__

N.C.

Es - pres - so,__

es - pres - so,__ es -

- pres - so,__ es - pres - so.__

There's a world

that we don't know,___ there's a world__ we ne - ver see.___

Es - pres - so,___ es - pres - so,___

es - pres - so,___ es - pres - so.___

Es - pres - so,___

es - pres - so,___   es -

- pres - so,___   es - pres - so.___

red

put your hand in the paintbox and choose
which one says the most about you
i would have to pick the deepest shade
the saddest shade of blue
but red is the colour i'd choose
oh red is the colour i'd choose

i set my soul long ago and far away
oh it's written down so deep
it can never fade away
though so many years have come and gone
through my life one thing has stayed
an eternal light that shines
clean through the grey

red is the colour i choose
deepest red in a sky of deepest blue
it don't matter now if i should win
if i should win or lose
'cause red is the colour i choose

if i waste my time away
waiting just for you
i don't care what the others say
'cause baby i just love
love what you do

red

Words & Music by
Chris Rea

26

I don't care what the oth-ers say __ 'cause ba-by I just a - love _____ love what you do.

Red is the co-lour I'd_ choose,_____ and deep-est red____ on a sky

of deep-est blue.___ And it don't,___ it don't mat-ter now,___ if I should win,

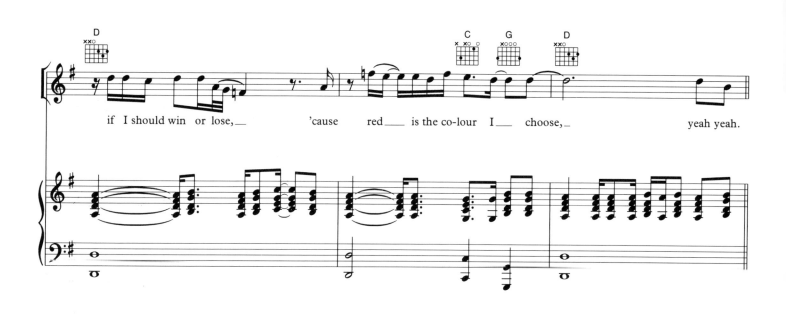

if I should win or lose,___ 'cause red___ is the co-lour I___ choose,___ yeah yeah.

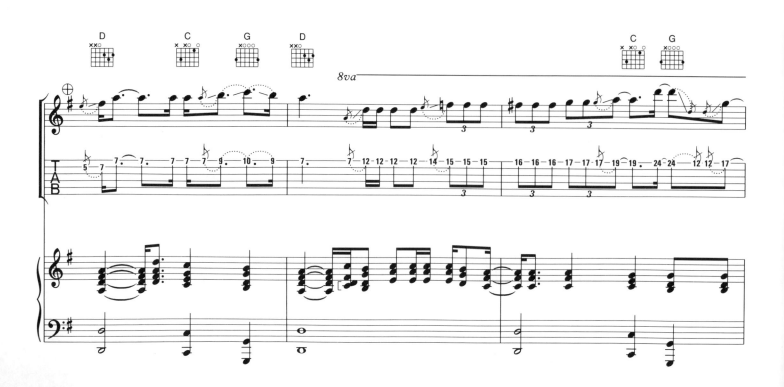

Well red is the co-lour I'd choose _____ yeah, deep-est red _____ on a sky

of deep - est blue. It don't mat-ter now, if I should win or

lose, 'cause red is the co-lour I'd choose.

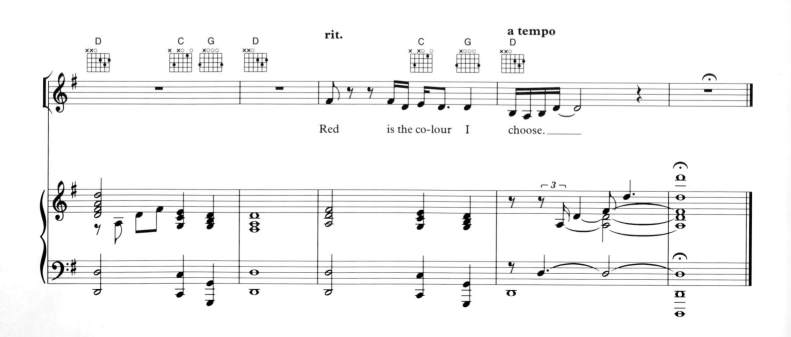

Red is the co-lour I choose.

soup of the day

well she thinks she's looking oh so cool
she thinks she's great
but she's just a fool
what awful lack of class
makes this kind behave this way
i look and only think
of one thing to say
soup, she's just soup, soup of the day

she's thin round the waistline
thin round the brain
you see this type so many times
time and time again
how could they really think
they'd be treated in any other way
everybody's looking and everybody say
soup, she's just soup, soup of the day

well you'd think that they'd know better
than behaving this way
they think they're being clever
but i really have to say
you'd better think it over
you'll regret it one fine day
when the circus party's over
you're just soup of the day
soup of the day

soup of the day

Words & Music by
Chris Rea

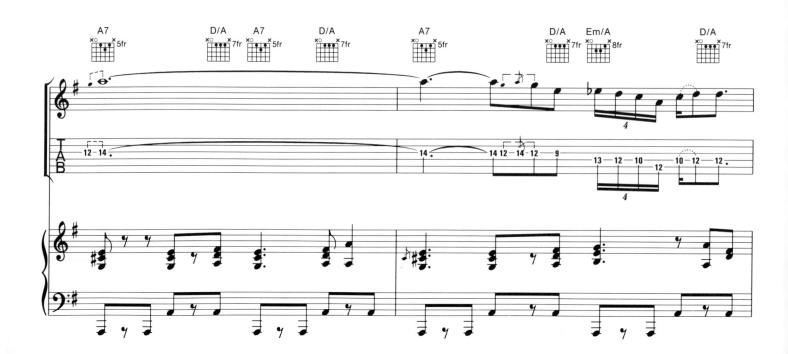

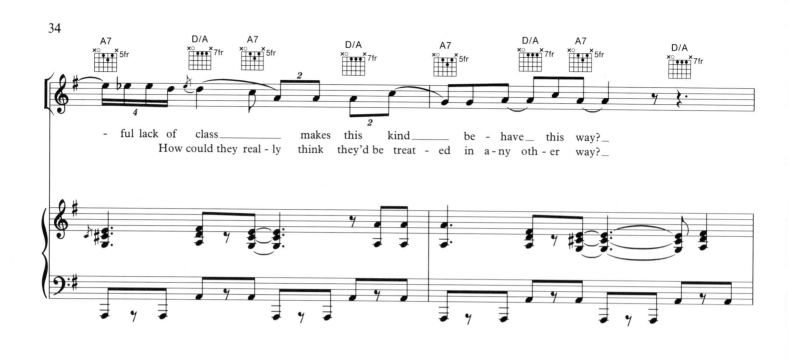

- ful lack of class_____ makes this kind_____ be - have__ this way?__
How could they real - ly think they'd be treat - ed in a - ny oth - er way?__

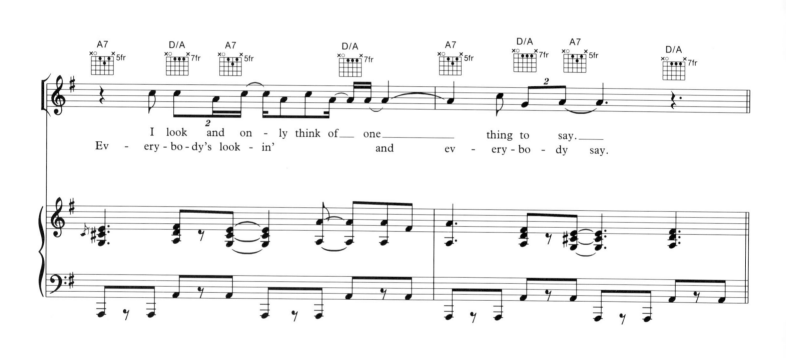

I look and on - ly think of__ one_____ thing to say.____
Ev - ery-bo-dy's look - in' and ev - ery-bo - dy say.

Soup, she's just soup,

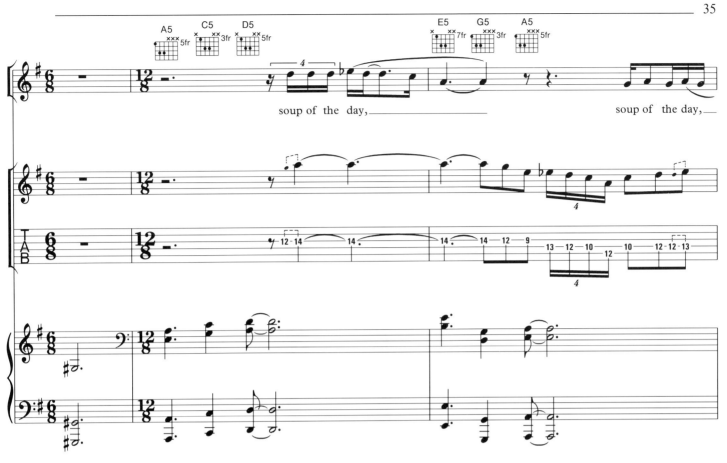

soup of the day,_____ soup of the day,___

_____ ooh, ooh.____ She's soup of the day.

here she comes now,_____ she just soup of the day___ uh, ooh.___

rit.

free time
A9

Soup of the day,_____ yeah.

johnny needs a fast car

johnny needs a fast car
johnny needs it bad
johnny always do the best
whatever johnny has
johnny needs a fast one
johnny needs it now
you got to give him something
to let him show you how

johnny needs a fast car
johnny needs a fast car

johnny needs a fast car
johnny needs a break
johnny don't need good luck
'cos johnny never fakes
he'll always make it look good
you'll always see him smile
give johnny a few inches
and he'll give you back a mile

johnny needs a fast car
johnny needs a fast car

tears upon the broken bones
of luck that never went his way
bless this one
you'll know him by his smile

johnny needs a fast car

Words & Music by
Chris Rea

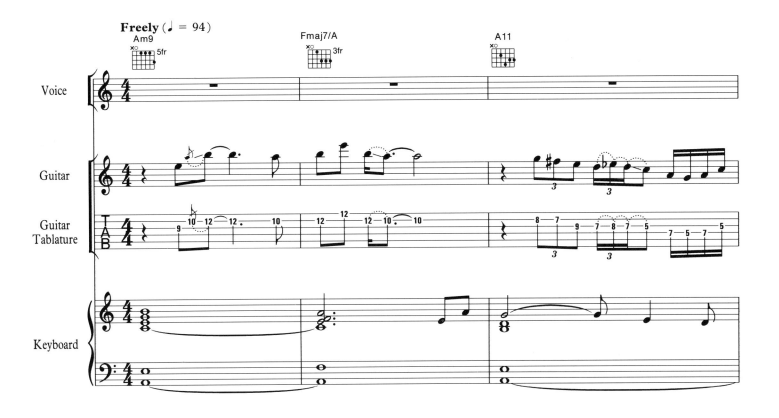

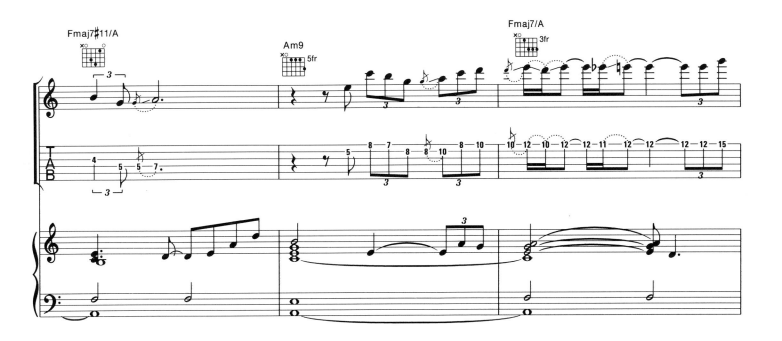

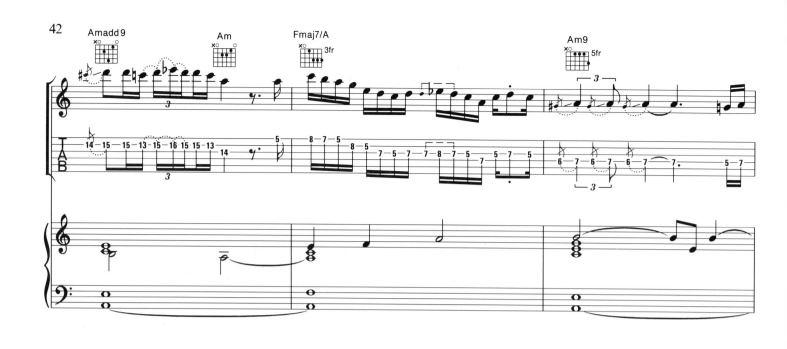

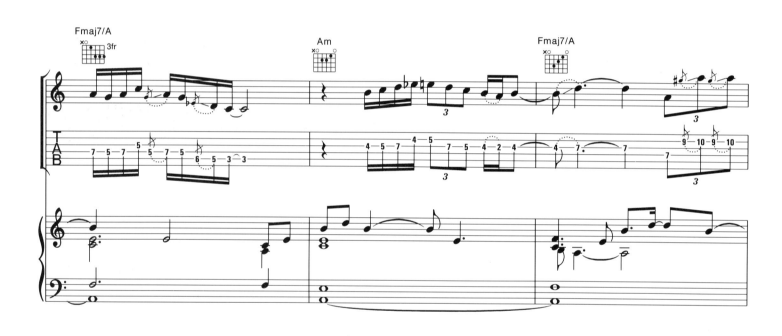

Johnny needs a fast car, Johnny needs it bad,
Johnny needs a fast car, Johnny needs a break,

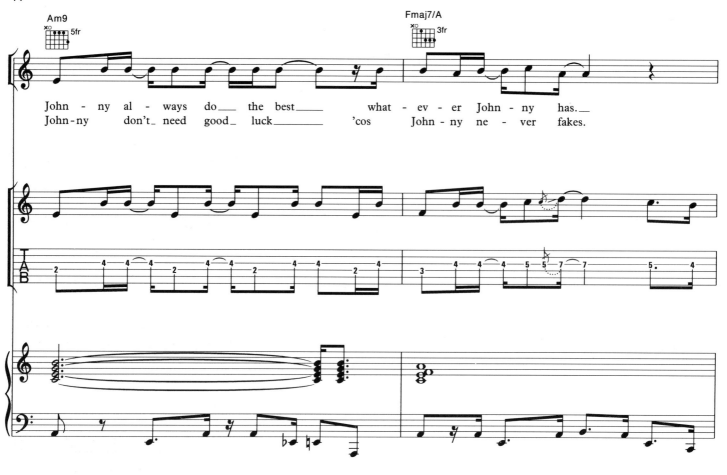

Johnny always do the best whatever Johnny has.
Johnny don't need good luck 'cos Johnny never fakes.

Johnny needs a fast one, Johnny needs it now, you
He'll always make it look good, you'll always see him smile, give

Tears up-on___ the bro-ken bones of luck___ that ne - ver went__ his way,__

bless this one,__ you'll know__ him by his smile._____

between the devil
and the deep blue sea

between the devil and the deep blue sea
everywhere i turn
it's got a hold on me
between the devil and the deep blue sea
everywhere i run
it won't let me be
caught between the devil and the deep blue sea

between the devil and the deep blue sea
can somebody somebody
somebody help me please
between the thunder
and the driving rain
could i ever be, be the same again
caught between the devil and the deep blue sea

holding on
waiting for some good luck to come
come my way
set me free

it's that old boy himself
and he always knew
sooner or later
if you don't say what's true
you'll end in chains
and you'll always be
caught between the devil and the deep blue sea

between the devil
and the deep blue sea

Words & Music by
Chris Rea

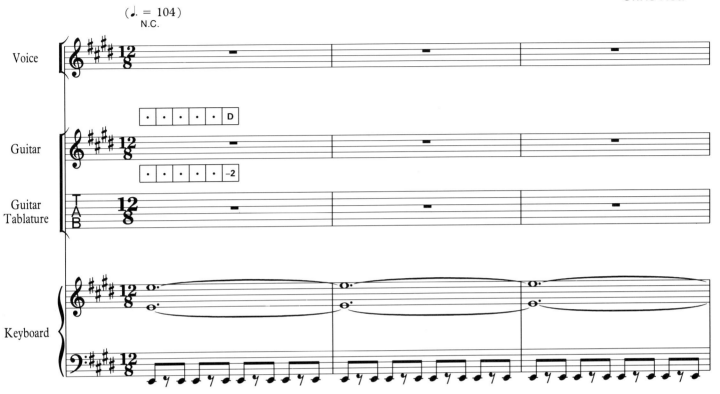

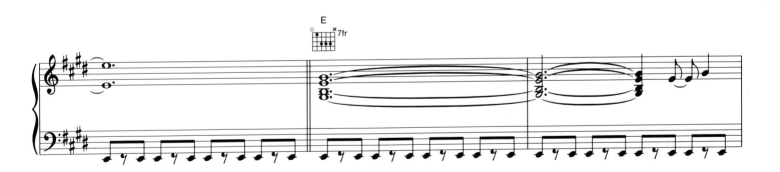

set me_ free.____

and the deep blue sea,_____ caught be-tween the de-

-vil_____ and the deep blue sea._____

repeat ad lib. to fade

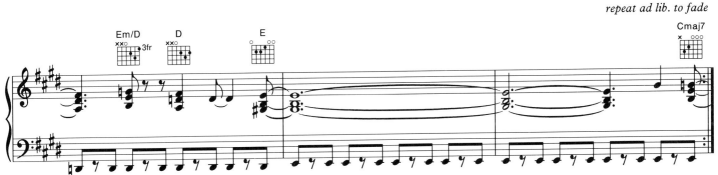

julia

eyes so bright
so big and wide
make you feel so strange
somewhere deep inside
it's the face of an angel
soul of the devil-may-care
i'd love to know
what goes on in there
she needs your love
she needs it every day
but speak of love
see her laugh and run away

julia, which way will you go
julia, i wanna know
julia, only the moon and stars
julia, know just where you are
julia

see the dance
that needs no alibi
you don't need to dream
when you know you can fly
she needs your love
she needs it every day
but speak of love
see her laugh and run away

julia, which way will you go
julia, i wanna know
julia, only the moon and stars
julia, know just where you are
julia

julia

Words & Music by
Chris Rea

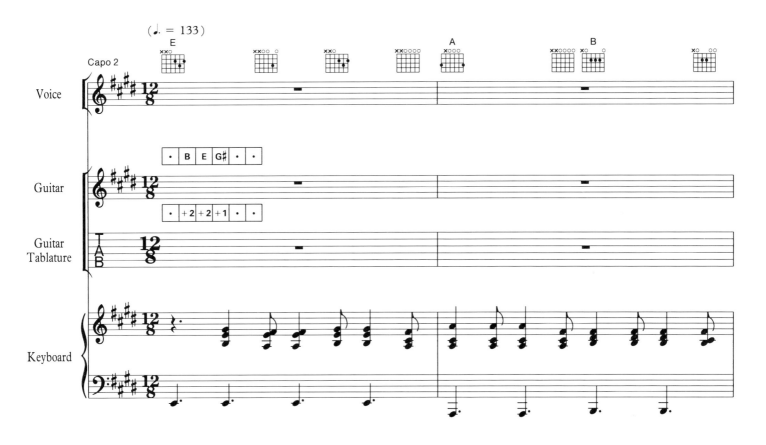

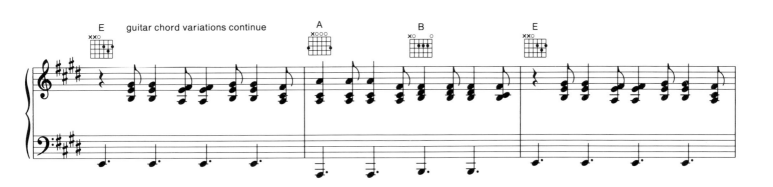

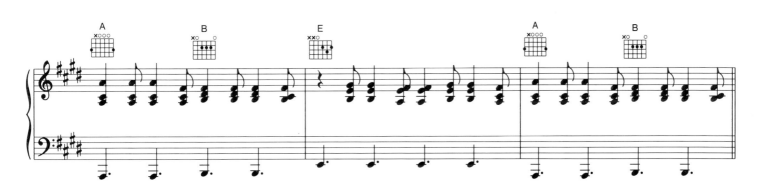

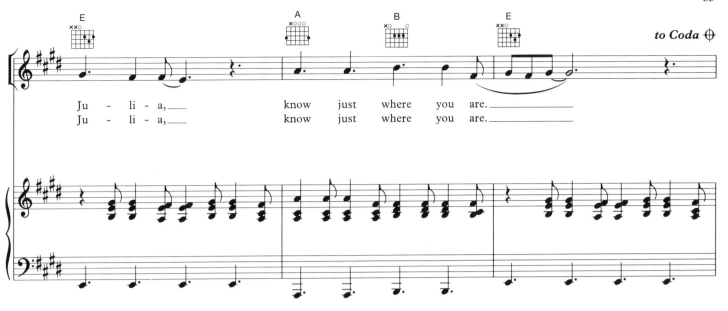

Ju - li - a,___ know just where you are._____
Ju - li - a,___ know just where you are._____

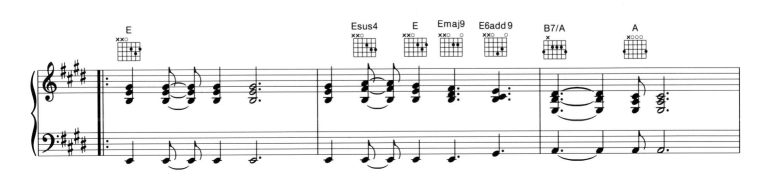

Ju - li - a,

D.𝄋 al Coda　　　　⊕ *CODA*

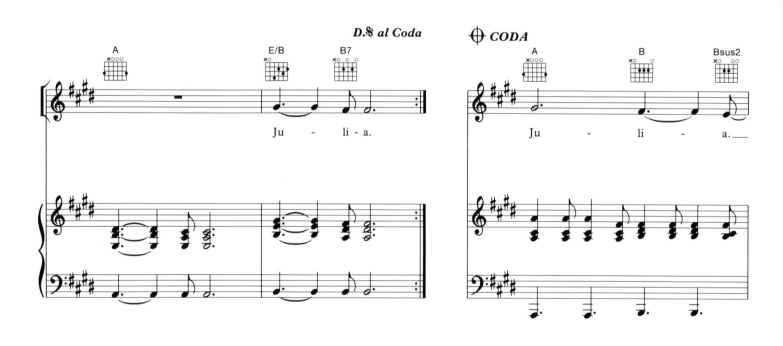

Ju - li - a.　　　　Ju - li - a. ___

summer love

once there was a summer love
long ago and far away
the autumn whispers to the falling leaves
summer love can't stay

this was their place this was where
just for one moment without cares
two lovers dream of how the world should be
please bring back my summer love to me

did you have to go
did i have to stay
did you have to go
away
now it's all gone
but who can forget
summer love
sweet summer love

i see your shadow everywhere
i feel your smile though you're not there
a kiss for every star in the sky way above
you'll always be my one and only
summer love

summer love

Words & Music by
Chris Rea

now it's all gone   but who can for-get   sum-mer love,   sweet sum-mer love?

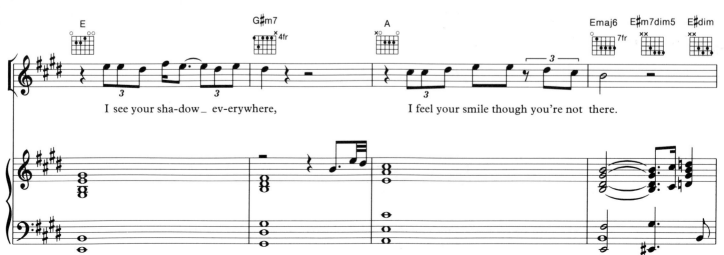

I see your sha-dow __ ev-erywhere,   I feel your smile though you're not there.

new way

i go to work in a bubble
i got everything i need
i get so high on no trouble
it's a great feeling being free

i say a prayer at thanksgiving
i bless the night and the day
i look to the sky with a smile on my face
and i praise the lord
of the new way

the sweetest sound i ever heard
was the sound of reason falling
like the summer rain
and the truth that washed the pain away
new way

i don't watch tv anymore
don't need to see it
now we all know the score
and all the politicians know
what they're there for
it's a new way

new way

Words & Music by
Chris Rea

of rea-son fall - ing___ like the sum - mer rain, and the

truth that washed the pain___ a - way.___

New   way,___   new___ way.

stop

gone too far
gone too long
messed it up completely
till everything is wrong
stop, start over, start again
you better stop, start over, start again

too many pieces
too much to chew
how can you ever win
when you're so scared to lose
you better stop, start over, start again
stop, start over, start again

walk away
see what it looks like from here
if you stay
you will only drown
in a mass of fear

you need to sleep
you need a break
you got to find out
before it gets too late
stop, start again
you better stop, start over, start again

.

stop

Words & Music by
Chris Rea

Gone too far,___ gone too long,___
Too ma-ny pie-ces, too much to chew,___

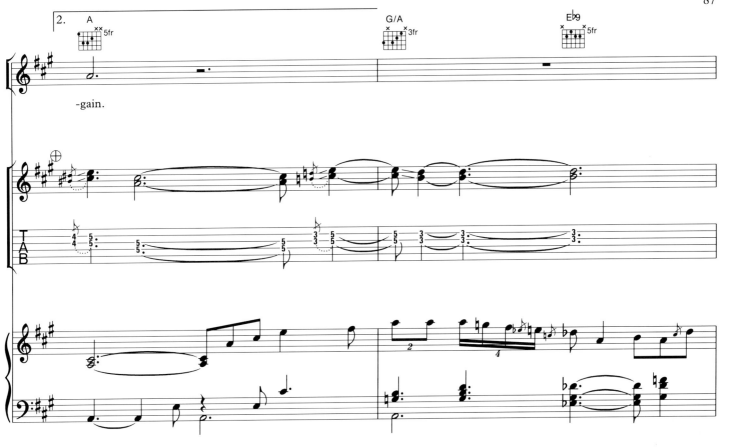

-gain.

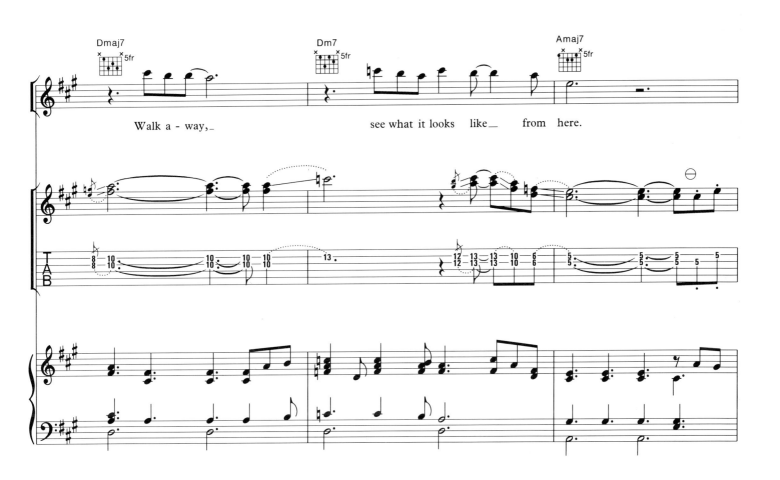

Walk a - way,___   see what it looks like___ from here.

If you stay_____

you will on - ly___ drown___ in a mass___ of fear.

Walk a - way,__ see what it looks like__ from here.

'Cause if__ you stay_____ you will on - ly__

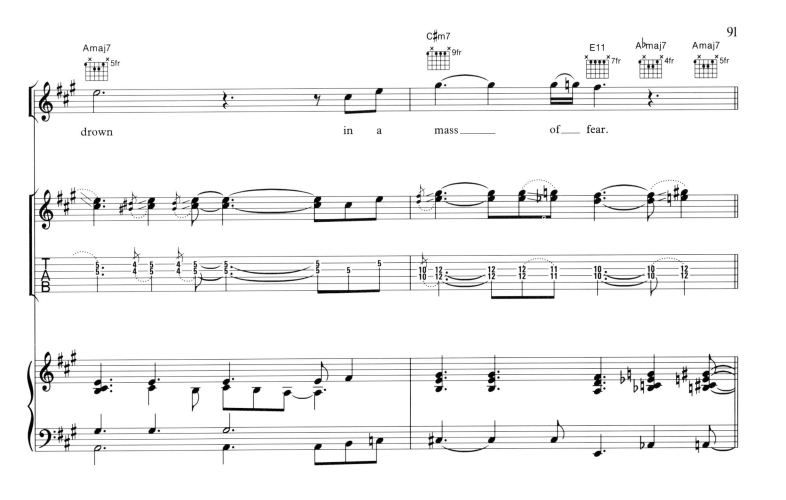

drown   in a mass___ of___ fear.

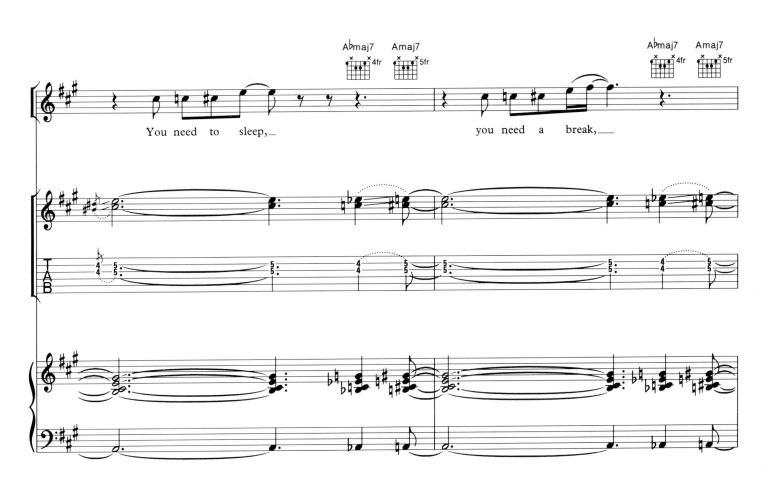

You need to sleep,___   you need a break,___

you got to find___ out___ be - fore it gets too late.___

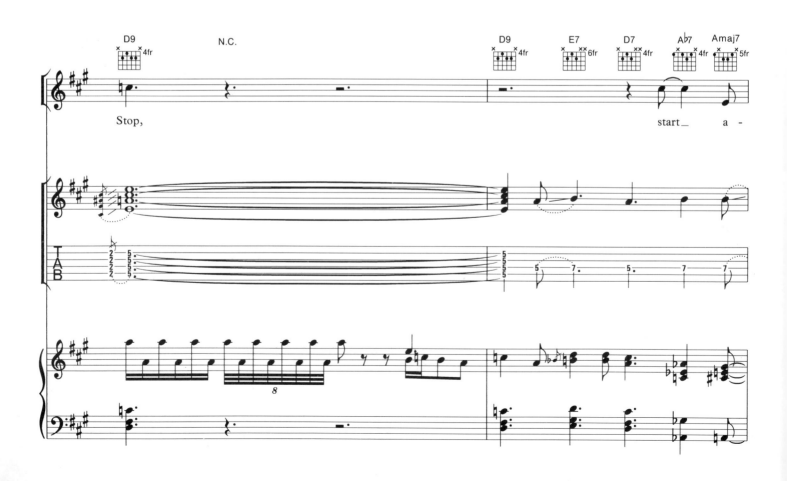

Stop,

start___ a -

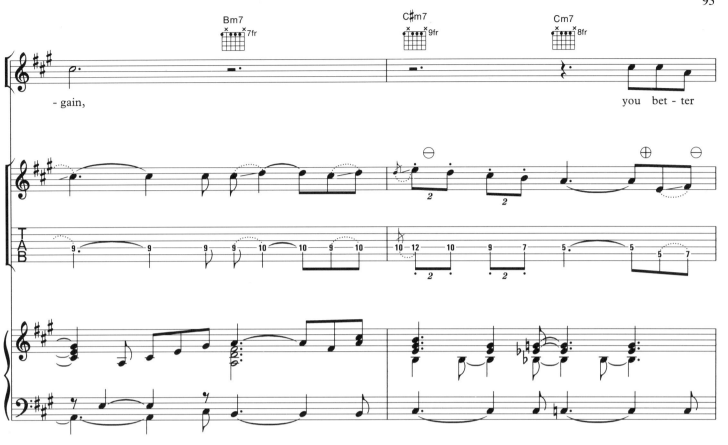

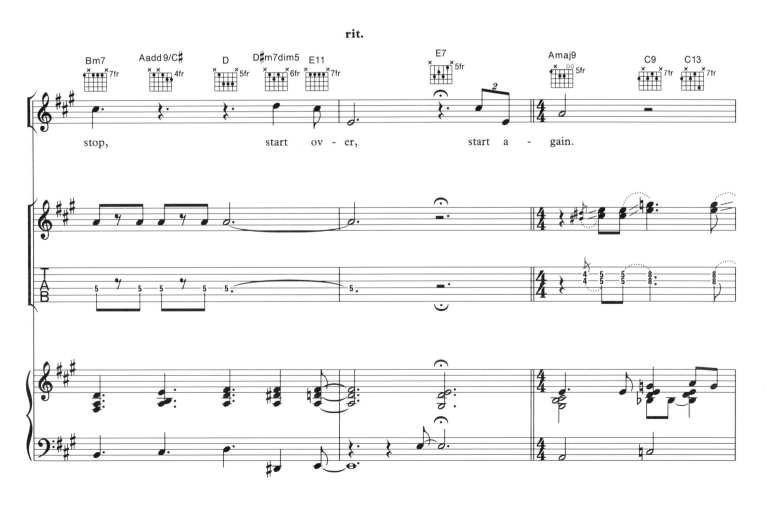

she closed her eyes

she closed her eyes
and let the walls of her prison fall away
the walls that ached with a timeless wait
that had become her walls
of this modern tv life
she closed her eyes
and let them fall away
and in her dreams
she is standing by an ocean
she is gazing out to sea
she can remember with just a fleeting glimpse
that she was once free
so long ago now
so long it was as if it had never been
was it a holiday
she thinks it could have been
ah, yes italy

and he closes his eyes
and he is gone far away
gone from all his confusion
gone from the pain
he can easily see what a pointless waste
his modern life has become
chasing the gravy train
chasing the dollar
chasing the clock
chasing his male friends
chasing the boss
chasing it like it was everything
it was nothing
only the sound of his own breathing
was all he really had
at the end of the day
and reasons to wonder
reasons to cry
too late for this selfish sinner
who never asked why

she closed her eyes

Words & Music by
Chris Rea

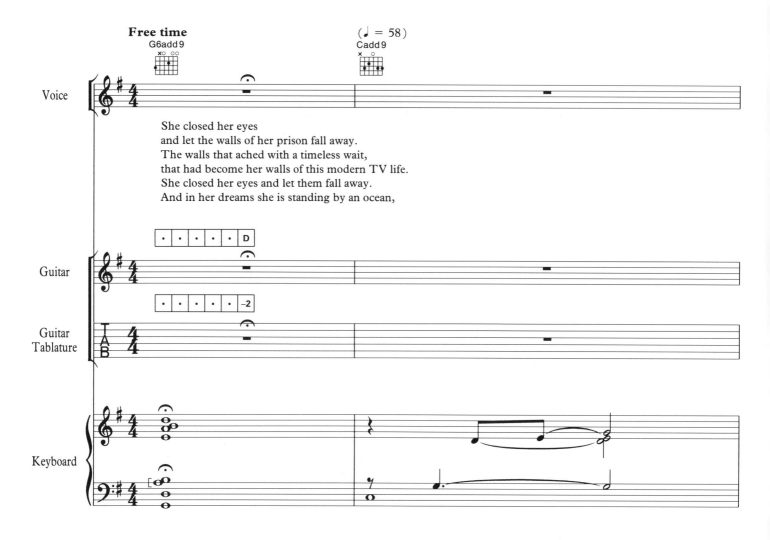

She closed her eyes
and let the walls of her prison fall away.
The walls that ached with a timeless wait,
that had become her walls of this modern TV life.
She closed her eyes and let them fall away.
And in her dreams she is standing by an ocean,

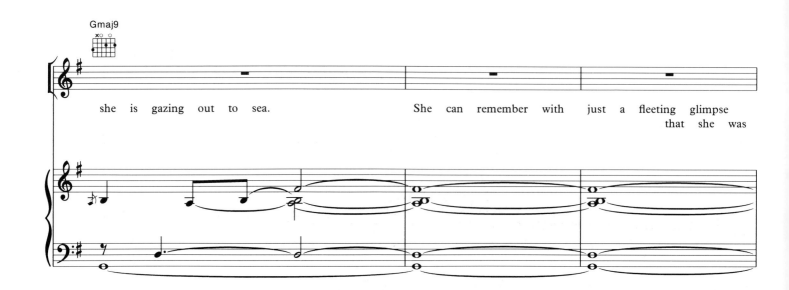

she is gazing out to sea.   She can remember with just a fleeting glimpse
that she was

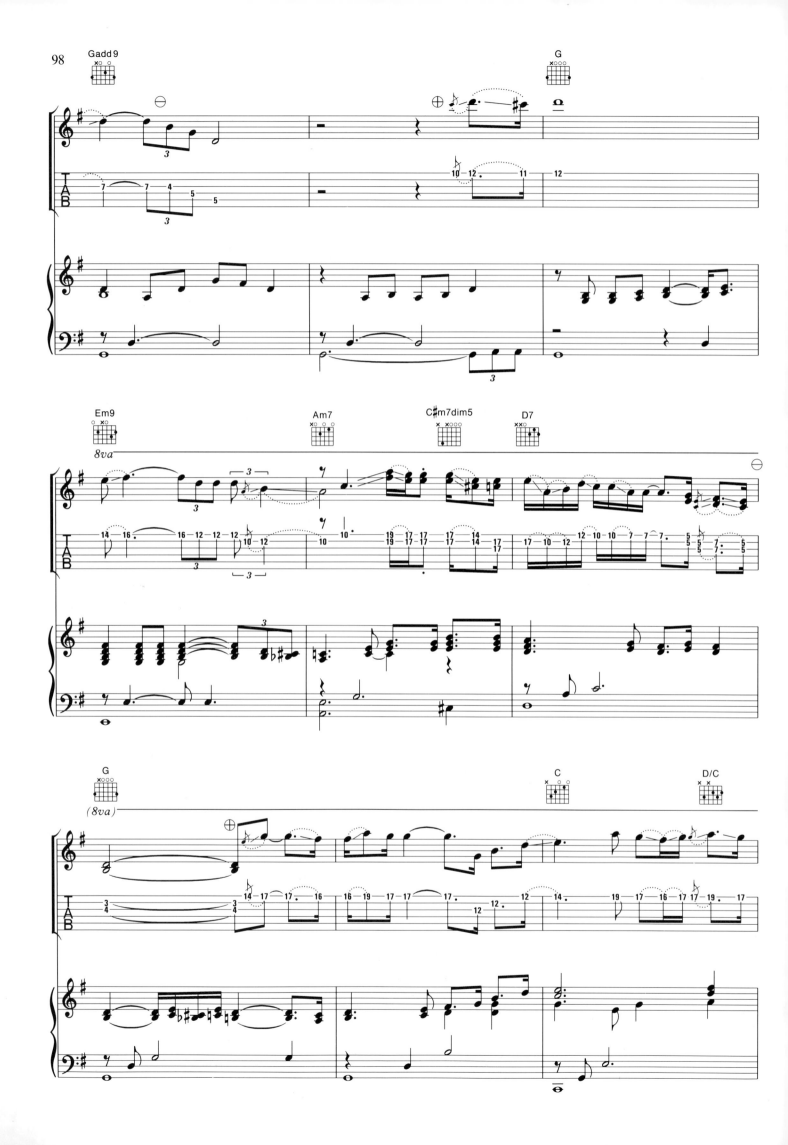

And he closes his eyes and he is gone far away gone from all his confusion,

gone from the pain. He can easily see what a pointless waste his modern life has become.

Indications sur la notation musicale et les tablatures

Accord de Do majeur ouvert

Gamme de Mi majeur

Mi aigu: 1ère corde
Si: 2e corde
Sol: 3e corde
Ré: 4e corde
La: 5e corde
Mi grave: 6e corde

Bending:

La note correspondant à la case sur laquelle on pose le doigt est toujours indiquée en premier. Les variations de hauteur sont obtenues en poussant sur la corde et sont indiquées par le symbole: ⌐⎺⌐ En cas de doute sur la hauteur à atteindre, le fait de jouer les notes indiquées sans pousser sur la corde permet de trouver ensuite la bonne hauteur. Les examples suivants démontrent les techniques de bending les plus courantes.

Exemple 1:
Jouez la note Ré et poussez la corde d'un ton (deux demi-tons) pour atteindre le Mi.

Exemple 4:
'Pre-bend': posez le doigt sur la case de Ré, poussez d'un ton pour atteindre le Mi avant de jouer la note.

Exemple 2:
Jouez le Ré, poussez sur la corde pour atteindre le Mi un ton plus haut, relâchez ensuite pour revenir au Ré. Seule la première note est jouée avec le médiator.

Exemple 5:
Jouez La et Ré simultanément; poussez ensuite sur la corde de Si pour atteindre la note Si.

Exemple 3:
'Fast Bend': jouez le Ré et poussez le plus rapidement possible pour atteindre le Mi.

Exemple 6:
Jouez Ré et Fa♯ simultanément; poussez la corde de Sol d'un ton vers le Mi, et la corde de Si d'un demi-ton vers le Sol.

D'autres techniques de guitare sont notées de la façon suivante:

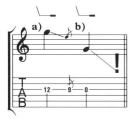

Emploi du levier de vibrato:
Modifiez la hauteur du son avec le levier de vibrato. Lorsque c'est possible, la note à atteindre est indiquée.
a) Jouez le Sol et appuyez sur le levier de vibrato pour atteindre le Mi.
b) Jouez un Sol à vide et détendez le plus possible la corde avec le levier de vibrato pour rendre un effect de 'bombe qui tombe' (divebomb).

Hammer On et Pull Off:
Jouez la première note; frappez la corde sur la touche (Hammer On) pour obtenir la seconde note, et relâchez la seconde note en tirant sur la corde (Pull Off) pour obtenir la troisième note. Seule la première note est donc jouée avec le médiator.

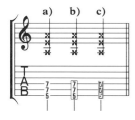

Mutes (étouffements):
a) Mute de la main droite:
Etouffez en posant la main droite sur les cordes, au-dessus du chevalet.
b) Mute de la main gauche:
Relâchez la pression sur la corde juste après avoir joué la note.
c) Mute sans hauteur définie:
Etouffez les cordes avec la main gauche pour obtenir un son de percussion.

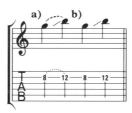

Glissando:
a) Jouez la première note avec le médiator, faites sonner la seconde note en ne faisant que glisser le doigt sur la corde.
b) Comme ci-dessus, mais en attaquant également la seconde note avec le médiator.

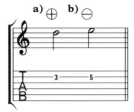

Guitare Slide:
a) Note jouée avec le slide.
b) Note jouée sans le slide.

Harmoniques naturelles:
Posez le doigt sur la corde au dessus de la barrette indiquée, et jouez avec le médiator pour obtenir un son cristallin. Le cas échéant, une petite note indique la hauteur du son que l'on doit obtenir.

Harmoniques pincées:
Appuyez le doigt sur la corde de la façon habituelle, mais utilisez conjointement le médiator et l'index de la main droite de façon á obtenir une harmonique aiguë. Les petites notes indiquent la hauteur du son que l'on doit obtenir.

Quarts de ton:
Une flèche dirigée vers le bas indique que la note est baissée d'un quart-de-ton. Une flèche dirigée vers le haut indique que la note est haussée d'un quart-de-ton.

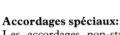

Accordages spéciaux:
Les accordages non-standards sont indiqués par six cases, chacune reprêsentant une corde (de gauche à droite), de la plus grave à la plus aiguê. Un tiret indique que la tension de la corde correspondante ne doit pas être altérée. Un nom de note indique la nouvelle note à obtenir. Pour les tablatures, les chiffres indiqués dans les cases représentent le nombre de demi-tons dont ou doit désaccorder la corde, vers le haut ou vers le bas.

Effet de Vibrato:
Jouez le vibrato soit avec le doigt sur la corde (main gauche), soit avec le levier de vibrato. Comme le vibrato est une affaire de technique et de goût personnels, il n'est indiqué que quand cela est vraiment nécessaire.

Harmoniques artificielles:
Posez le doigt (main gauche) sur la note la plus basse: effleurez la corde avec l'index de la main droite au-dessus de la barrette indiquée par la note en forme de losange, tout en actionnant le médiator. La petite note indique la hauteur du son que l'on doit obtenir.

Scratch:
Faites glisser le médiator du haut en bas de la corde. Le meilleur effet est obtenu avec des cordes filetées.

Accords répétés:
Pour faciliter la lecture des parties de guitare rythmique, les chiffres de tablature sont omis quand l'accord est répété. L'example montre successivement un accord de Do majeur joué de façon normale, un 'mute' de la main droite, un 'mute' de la main gauche et un 'mute' sans hauteur définie.

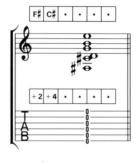

Accordez la corde de Mi grave un ton plus haut de façon à obtenir un Fa♯, et la corde de La deux tons plus haut de façon à obtenir un Do♯.

Noms des accords:

Les symboles standards utilisés pour les accords représentent l'harmonie principale, parfois simplifiée, et ne sont pas sensés indiquer l'accompagnement exact. Dans le chiffrage, les quintes altérées sont indiquées par 'dim5' et 'aug5', alors que les altérations des extensions de l'accord sont indiquées par un dièse ou un bémol.

Lorsqu'aucun nom d'accord précis n'est applicable, par exemple quand la musique consiste en une figure répétée (riff), le centre tonal est indiqué entre parenthèses.

Lorsqu'un passage n'a pas pu être transcrit, le symbole ∿ apparait.

Les voix féminines sont écrites à la bonne hauteur, les voix masculines sont transposées une octave plus haut qu'elles ne doivent être chantées.

Hinweise zu Notation und Tabulatur

Offener C - Dur - Akkord

E - Dur - Tonleiter

Hohe E-Saite (1.)
H-Saite (2.)
G-Saite (3.)
D-Saite (4.)
A-Saite (5.)
Tiefe E-Saite (6.)

Gezogene Noten:

Die gegriffene Note wird immer zuerst angegeben. Das Zeichen ⌐¯¯⌐ zeigt eine Veränderung der Tonhöhe an, die durch das Ziehen der Saiten erreicht wird. Falls Du nicht sicher bist, wie weit die Saite gezogen werden soll, spiele die entsprechenden Töne zunächst ohne Ziehen; so kannst Du Dich an der Tonhöhe orientieren. Die folgenden Beispiele geben die gebräuchlichsten Techniken zum Ziehen wieder:

Beispiel 1:
Spiele das D und ziehe dann um einen Ton (zwei Halbtonschritte) höher zum E.

Beispiel 2:
Spiele das D, ziehe um einen Ton hoch zum E und dann wieder zurück, so daß D erklingt. Dabei wird nur die erste Note angeschlagen.

Beispiel 3:
Schnelles Ziehen: Spiele das D und ziehe dann so schnell Du kannst um einen Ton höher zum E.

Beispiel 4:
Im Voraus gezogen: Greife das D, ziehe um einen Ton höher zum E und schlage erst dann die Saite an.

Beispiel 5:
Spiele A und D gleichzeitig und ziehe dann die H-Saite um einen Ton nach oben, so daß H erklingt.

Beispiel 6:
Spiele D und Fis gleichzeitig; ziehe dann die G-Saite um einen Ton nach oben zum E und die H-Saite um einen Halbtonschritt nach oben zum G.

Zusätzliche Spieltechniken für Gitarre wurden folgendermaßen notiert:

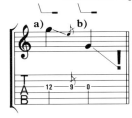

Tremolo:
Verändere die Tonhöhe mit dem Tremolo-Hebel. Wenn es möglich ist, wird die angestrebte Tonhöhe angezeigt.
a) Spiele G; nutze den Takt, um zum E abzusteigen.
b) Spiele die leere G-Saite; nutze den Takt, um so weit wie möglich abzusteigen.

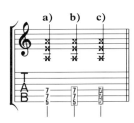

Dämpfen:
a) Mit der rechten Hand:
Dämpfe die Saiten, indem Du die rechte Hand einfach oberhalb der Brücke auf die Saiten legst.
b) Mit der linken Hand:
Dämpfe die Saiten, indem Du den Druck der linken Hand löst, kurz nachdem die Töne erklingen.
c) Ohne bestimmte Tonhöhe:
Dämpfe die Saiten mit der linken Hand; so erzielst Du einen 'geschla--genen' Sound.

Hammer on und Pull off:
Spiele die erste Note; die zweite erklingt durch 'Hammering on', die dritte durch 'Pulling off'. Dabei wird nur die erste Note angeschlagen.

Glissando:
a) Spiele die erste Note; die zweite erklingt durch Hochrutschen des Fingers auf der Saite. Nur die erste Note wird angeschlagen.
b) Wie oben, aber die zweite Note wird angeschlagen.

Slide Guitar:
a) Spiele mit Rutschen des Fingers.
b) Spiele ohne Rutschen.

Vibrato:
Beim Vibrato läßt Du die Note für die Dauer eines Tons durch Druck--variation oder Tremolo-Hebel 'beben'. Da es jedoch eine Frage des persönlichen Geschmacks ist, wird Vibrato nur dort angegeben, wo es unerläßlich ist.

Natürliches Flageolett:
Berühre die Saite über dem angegebenen Bund; wenn Du jetzt anschlägst, entsteht ein glockenähnlicher Ton. Wo es nötig ist, zeigen kleine Notenköpfe die entstandene Note an.

Künstliches Flageolett:
Greife die unterste Note, berühre die Saite über dem durch Rauten angegebenen Bund und schlage dann den Ton an. Die kleinen Noten--köpfe zeigen wieder die entstandene Note an.

Gezupftes Flageolett:
Greife die Note ganz normal, aber drücke die Saite mit der zupfenden Hand so, daß ein harmonischer Oberton entsteht. Kleine Notenköpfe zeigen den entstandenen Ton an.

Pick Scratch:
Fahre mit dem Plektrum nach unten über die Saiten – das klappt am besten bei umsponnenen Saiten.

Vierteltöne:
Ein nach unten gerichteter Pfeil bedeutet, daß die notierte Tonhöhe um einen Viertelton erniedrigt wird; ein nach oben gerichteter Pfeil bedeutet, daß die notierte Tonhöhe um einen Viertelton erhöht wird.

Akkordwiederholung:
Um die Stimmen für Rhyth--mus-Gitarre leichter lesbar zu machen, werden die Tabulaturziffern weggelassen, wenn ein Akkord wiederholt werden soll. Unser Beispiel zeigt einen C - Dur - Akkord normal gespielt, rechts gedämpft, links gedämpft und ohne Tonhöhe.

Besondere Stimmung:
Falls eine Stimmung verlangt wird, die vom Standard abweicht, wird sie in Kästchen angegeben. Jedes Kästchen steht für eine Saite, das erste links außen entspricht der tiefsten Saite. Wenn die Tonhöhe einer Saite nicht verändert werden soll, enthält das Kästchen einen Punkt. Steht eine Note im Kästchen, muß die Saite wie angegeben umgestimmt werden. In der Tabulatur--schrift stehen stattdessen Ziffern im entsprechenden Kästchen: Sie geben die Zahl der Halbtonschritte an, um die eine Saite höher oder tiefer gestimmt werden soll.

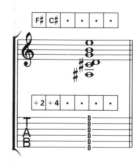

Stimme die tiefe E-Saite (6.) um einen Ganzton (zwei Halbtonschritte) höher auf Fis und die A-Saite (5.) um zwei Ganztöne (vier Halbtonschritte) höher auf Cis.

Akkordbezeichnung:
Die folgenden Akkordbezeichnungen wurden verwendet. Allerdings stehen die Akkordsymbole (manchmal vereinfacht) für die Grundharmonie; sie sind also nicht dafür gedacht, eine genaue Begleitung zu ermöglichen. Alterierte Quinten werden mit 'dim5' oder 'aug5' bezeichnet, während Alterationen von hinzugefügten Noten durch '♯' oder '♭' angegeben sind.

Wenn kein eigenes Akkordsymbol angegeben ist, z.B. bei Wiederholung einer musikalischen Figur (bzw. Riff), steht die Harmoniebezeichnung in Klammern: **[E]**

Das Symbol ∼ steht jeweils dort, wo es nicht möglich war, einen Abschnitt zu übertragen.

Frauenstimmen sind im Original angegeben, Männerstimmen eine Oktave höher als gesungen.

Printed in England
Panda Press · Haverhill · Suffolk • 3/94